This book was presented to

The Eliot Montessori School

by. Mehar reddy Poreddy

on. MaY 14 2010

The Sydney Opera House

by Peggy J. Parks

BLACKBIRCH®
PRESS

San Diego • Detroit • New York • San Francisco • Cleveland • New Haven, Conn. • Waterville, Maine • London • Munich

THOMSON

GALE

For more information, contact
The Gale Group, Inc.
27500 Drake Rd.
Farmington Hills, MI 48331-3535
Or you can visit our Internet site at http://www.gale.com

LIBRARY OF CONGRESS CATALOGING-IN-PUBLICATION DATA

Parks, Peggy J.
  The Sydney Opera House / by Peggy J. Parks.
    p. cm. — (Building world landmarks)
Includes bibliographical references and index.
  ISBN 1-4103-0447-7 (hardback : alk. paper)
  1. Sydney Opera House (Australia)—History—Juvenile literature. I. Title. II.
Series.

Printed in the United States
10 9 8 7 6 5 4 3 2 1

Table of Contents

Introduction
A Building Ahead of Its Time 5

Chapter 1
In Search of the Perfect Design 9

Chapter 2
Never-Ending Hurdles 17

Chapter 3
A Stunning Building Comes to Life 23

Chapter 4
Stops and Starts 31

Chapter 5
Australia's Dream Becomes a Reality 39

Notes 44

Chronology 45

Glossary 46

For More Information 47

About the Author 47

Index 48

A Building Ahead of Its Time

IN THE SOUTHERN hemisphere, the area of the earth below the equator, lies the country of Australia. Often called "the land down under," Australia is unique because not only is it a country, it is also a continent as well as an island. Visitors have long been drawn to this mysterious land, intriguing because of its natural beauty. Yet one of Australia's most famous landmarks is not a product of nature at all. It is the Sydney Opera House, one of the most stunning human-made structures in the world.

Located in the southeastern Australian territory of New South Wales, the Sydney Opera House has been called one of the Seven Wonders of the Modern World. With the water of Sydney Harbor on three sides and the grass and trees of the Royal Botanic Gardens on its fourth side, it stands completely clear of any other buildings. Each year thousands of people

Opposite:
As shown in this aerial photograph, the Sydney Opera House is surrounded by Sydney Harbor on three sides and the Royal Botanic Gardens on the fourth.

The soaring roof of the Opera House, covered with more than a million ceramic tiles, looks like an enormous ship at full sail.

stand in awe of the majestic, towering building that resembles an enormous ship at full sail. Architects and engineers worldwide marvel at the structure that covers nearly five acres of land and weighs 355 million pounds (161 million kilograms). Its distinctive, soaring shell-like roofs are covered with more than a million

Swedish ceramic tiles, with the biggest roof section towering 221 feet (67 meters) above sea level—taller than a twenty-story building.

Nowhere on earth is there anything quite like the Sydney Opera House. It holds a prominent place among the great buildings of the world, and that prominence is described by Richard Weston, an architecture professor from Wales (United Kingdom), who said: "As an icon, it rivals the Eiffel Tower, Taj Mahal and the Pyramids and its profile must be almost as familiar as Muhammad Ali's face or a Coca-Cola bottle."[1]

The Sydney Opera House has almost a thousand rooms and presents more than two thousand performances every year.

Chapter 1

In Search of the Perfect Design

LONG BEFORE SYDNEY had any type of performing arts center, a man named Eugene Goossens dreamed of such a place. A violinist and conductor from England, Goossens was hired in 1946 to lead the Sydney Symphony Orchestra. When he arrived, however, an unpleasant surprise awaited him. There was no concert hall in Sydney, or even a decent-sized theater, and orchestra performances were held in the town hall. Because he believed that music should reach out to all people, he resolved that a performance center would be built.

A Slow Start

Yet as much as Goossens wanted the facility, winning the government's approval was no easy task. For the next six years no progress was made, but he would not give up. To build public awareness about the project,

Opposite:
More than two hundred architects from around the world vied for the chance to design the performing arts center at Sydney Harbor's Bennelong Point.

Goossens gave radio addresses and often talked to the media. Then, in the fall of 1954, he met with Australian premier John Joseph Cahill, who expressed his support of Goossens's idea. Cahill appointed a committee to investigate having an opera house built.

The committee's first task was to select a location, and they chose a peninsula on Sydney Harbor called Bennelong Point. They determined that the facility should include one large theater (or hall) and another smaller one, as well as a restaurant and various other rooms and studios. Once these criteria were finalized, the committee planned a design competition that would be open to architects throughout the world. The entries would be judged by four men, all of whom were highly respected members of the architectural profession.

The Winning Design

In January 1956, the government announced the competition, which attracted enormous interest among architects from all over the world. There were 233 entries from Australia, Germany, the United States, Japan, and other countries. The judging took place in January 1957, and at the end of that month, Cahill publicly announced the winner: Jørn Utzon, a relatively unknown architect from Denmark.

Most people were surprised that Utzon had won, and some were shocked. His design was highly unusual, unlike anything they had ever seen before. A huge open staircase reached from a ground-level concourse to the top level of a massive tiered platform, called a

podium. On top of the podium sat three buildings—
two theaters side by side and a restaurant in front of
them—without traditional walls or roofs. Instead, the
structures were enclosed by vast curtains of glass attached to a series of interlocking shells that rested on
the podium, soared high into the air, and fanned out
like the sails of a ship.

In addition to the unusual nature of Utzon's design,
there was another reason people were surprised that
he won: he had not followed the competition rule that
specified "working drawings," which meant all details

*Jørn Utzon, an
architect from
Denmark, won
the design
competition
even though his
drawings were
incomplete.*

were to be completely worked out. Utzon's drawings were not only incomplete, they were quite rough. The judges, though, believed his entry was clearly the best— yet their statement to the media had a cautionary tone: "Because of its very originality, it is clearly a controversial design. However, we are absolutely convinced of its merits."[2] In addition to winning a cash prize, Utzon was appointed by the New South Wales government as the lead architect for the opera house.

Moving Forward

Utzon traveled to Australia in July 1957, and after one look at Bennelong Point, he enthusiastically approved of the site. He attended meetings in Sydney and then returned to Denmark. Over the next few months, he reviewed his plans with specialized consultants in order to identify any construction issues or concerns. Some of his meetings were with Ove Arup and Partners, a well-known London firm that was chosen to provide consulting engineers for the opera house project.

By the time Utzon returned to Sydney in the spring of 1958, he had refined his designs and prepared a brochure for Cahill and the opera house committee. This "Red Book" contained plans and sketches, as well as comments by the consultants with whom Utzon had conferred. The most pressing issue pointed out by Ove Arup was the massive shell-like roof—specifically, whether it would be structurally sound. As a seasoned engineer, Arup knew the roof needed to withstand the strong winds of Sydney Harbor, and his concerns were clearly spelled out in Utzon's brochure.

Bennelong

During the seventeenth century, Europeans frequently visited the site of present-day Sydney. In 1770, explorer Captain James Cook claimed the entire east coast of Australia for England's King George III, calling it New South Wales.

In 1786, British navy captain Arthur Phillip was appointed to be the first governor of New South Wales. At that time, England lacked sufficient space to house its many prisoners, and the government sought a new place where convicts could be sent. A year later, Phillip sailed to the new territory with a fleet of ships. On January 18, 1788, the fleet reached an area that Phillip later named Sydney Cove. With a total of 759 male and female convicts, 13 of the convicts' children, 206 marines, their wives and children, and 20 British officials, Phillip established a new settlement and named it Sydney.

The land was inhabited by Aborigines, native Australian people who had lived there for thousands of years. Phillip wanted to establish good relations with the natives. Because the Aborigines spoke a language he did not understand, this was difficult, so Phillip took the radical step of capturing several of them. His intent was not to harm them, but to find a way to establish communication between

Bennelong, an Aborigine, bridged communication between his people and the British.

the natives and the colonists. One of the captured men was named Bennelong.

Bennelong turned out to be highly intelligent, personable, and clever. He escaped after six months, but then cautiously returned, trusting that Phillip's motive was not to hold him and other Aborigines as prisoners. The two became friends, and Bennelong quickly learned enough English to become Phillip's interpreter.

In 1792 Phillip returned to England, and Bennelong accompanied him. In 1795, Bennelong traveled back to Sydney. He died in 1813. Years later, the peninsula that stretched into Sydney Harbor was named Bennelong Point in the aboriginal man's honor.

The tram shed, seen here in 1957, was torn down in 1958 to make way for the new opera house.

Full Steam Ahead

By mid-1958, drawings for the opera house were not yet complete and there were still major issues to address, but Cahill wanted construction to begin anyway. He was convinced that if work was held up until every problem was solved, there would never be an opera house. He was also worried that some political opponents who had spoken out against the project would try to stop it—and he had no intention of letting that happen.

Cahill's confidence, in part, was due to a major hurdle he had overcome a year before when he figured out how to finance the opera house. He had proposed the idea of a state lottery, whereby tickets would be sold to the public for three dollars each.

Lottery winners would win cash prizes, and the money left over would be more than enough to pay the $7 million in construction costs that Cahill had estimated. Government officials had approved the lottery and now, against the advice of both Utzon and Arup, Cahill pressed the opera house committee for approval to move ahead with the project.

And So It Begins

Cahill's persistence paid off, and the committee agreed to a compromise: Construction could begin but it would be divided into three separate stages, which meant some work could be started while plans for later work were still being developed. The podium, grand staircase, and concourse would be constructed during the first stage; the roof would be built during stage two; and the glass walls and interior work would be completed during stage three.

In August 1958, wrecking crews began to demolish an old tram shed on Bennelong Point to make way for the opera house. On March 2, 1959, Cahill and Utzon presided over a ceremony to mark the start of construction. The opera house, which had been nothing but a dream for many years, was finally going to be built.

There were two people, however, who never lived to see it. Eugene Goossens, the man determined to bring music to the people of Sydney, had returned to his native England where he later died. And John Joseph Cahill, who fought to keep the opera house dream alive, died just seven months after the groundbreaking ceremony.

Never-Ending Hurdles

WITHIN DAYS OF the groundbreaking, building crews moved onto Bennelong Point. A contract for the first stage had been awarded to Civil & Civic Contractors, an Australian construction firm. Yet before they could even begin, a problem was discovered that caused additional cost and schedule delays.

Problems from the Ground Up

At the time the opera house was being designed, it was assumed that Bennelong Point sat on the same compact sandstone that lay beneath most of Sydney. Then engineers bored into the earth and discovered loose sedimentary rock instead of sandstone. For the ground to support such a heavy structure, major reinforcements were necessary. Around the perimeter of the site, workers drilled seven hundred holes into solid bedrock. Then they sank thick steel and concrete

Opposite: Although construction began in early 1959, it took almost four years just to build the podium—the building's primary foundation.

beams into the holes. In the center, where the bulk of the building would sit, they poured a massive concrete slab to replace the unstable ground.

Another problem faced by workers was not having complete drawings, which caused inefficiency as well as delays. Construction was underway, but Utzon and Arup engineers were still working out many of the podium's details. As a result, they handed plans over to crews on a piecemeal basis rather than giving them complete drawings all at once.

The Great Podium Takes Shape

Despite the incomplete drawings, workers were under pressure to get the podium built because it served as the building's primary foundation. They started by

By the time it was finished, the concrete podium covered four and a half acres of land. Twenty reinforced pillars served as structural supports for the walls and roof.

building formwork (or molds) out of plywood and steel reinforcing bar, and then poured concrete into the molds to shape the floors and walls. Once the concrete had hardened, workers removed the formwork and the platform stood on its own—a massive structure as big as three football fields. The upper level, which was scooped out to accommodate theater seating, would house the two primary theaters, with the stage areas and main foyers between them. The smaller drama theater, as well as numerous other rooms and halls, would be inside the podium.

On the landward side of Bennelong Point, construction crews built an open staircase that stretched from the ground level to the top of the podium. The staircase was huge—more than 280 feet (85 meters) wide and 600 feet (183 meters) deep from front to back. A large concrete concourse was built under the staircase to provide access to cars and buses dropping passengers off in front of the opera house. (No parking would be permitted on the opera house grounds.) Workers built a pedestrian walkway known as a broadwalk, circling the other three sides of the building. The walk would allow theatergoers to stroll around and enjoy the harbor view.

As work progressed on the podium, Utzon and Arup continued to finalize the details of the immense roof—and it was an unbelievably tough challenge. No building in the world had a roof as big or as intricate as the one designed by Utzon. Moreover, in his quest to create a look of free-form sculpture, Utzon had not defined the roof shells by giving them fixed shapes or exact dimensions. He had also envisioned the shells as just a few inches thick, but Arup determined that this would cause the roof to be extremely vulnerable to high winds. It needed to be much stronger and heavier than Utzon originally planned.

This uncertainty about the size and weight of the roof presented yet another major problem for construction crews. No matter what the roof ended up looking like, the podium had to be built to accommodate it. Relying solely on sketchy plans provided by Arup, Civil & Civic estimated how heavy the roof would be. Then they built twenty reinforced concrete pillars on the podium that would function as structural supports. These pillars were positioned in the areas of the large theater, small theater, and restaurant, where the large concrete roof sections would be built.

A New Solution—a New Problem

It took four years for crews to finish building the podium. When it was finished in 1963, it covered four and a half acres of land—almost every inch of Bennelong Point. Next on the schedule was the roof, and after years of seemingly impossible options, Utzon finally had the answer. Instead of the shells being completely free-form, with each section different from the others, they would all be part of the same sphere—different sizes but identical in form. (Utzon compared these sections to the segments of a peeled orange.) This revised design would make it easier to calculate the precise shape and dimensions of each roof section, which Arup measured by using computers. Also,

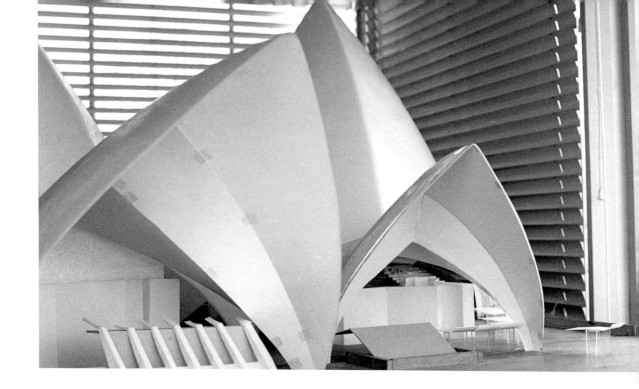

Utzon redesigned the shells to be much thicker so they could stand up to the wind.

This change solved the roof problem, but it also radically changed the weight. Now the shells would be a great deal heavier than previously thought, so workers had to build twelve more supportive pillars. In addition, the twenty existing pillars were no longer strong enough—and changing them was not as simple as adding concrete to make them thicker. The pillars had to be demolished and completely rebuilt. Workers did this by drilling holes in the center of each pillar, filling the holes with explosive material, and blowing off the concrete. Once the steel centers were left bare, bigger forms were built around them, and new concrete was poured into the forms. After the concrete had hardened, the forms were removed, and the pillars stood ready to support the building's immense roof.

This model of the opera house shows the roof's shells, which had to be redesigned to withstand the strong harbor winds.

A Stunning Building Comes to Life

IN THE FALL of 1962, an Australian firm, the Horni-brook Group, was chosen to build the opera house roof. There would be three main sections, known as roof vaults, that would tower above the two halls and the restaurant. The vaults would be made up of fan-shaped concrete shells that curved toward each other, forming a series of graceful arches.

Towering Shells

Because of the immense size and weight of the roof, Arup determined that it should not be constructed the traditional way, which was for workers to build it while balancing on tall metal platforms called scaffold-ing. Instead, they built individual roof segments on the ground and then assembled them. Scaffolding was still needed, and workers built it to use for the final

Opposite:
The Sydney Opera House glows at sunset. Utzon special-ordered tiles from Sweden to ensure the roof would reflect light and glimmer in the dark.

roof construction; however, the bulk of the work would not have to be done from high in the air.

The first step was to make molds—curved, to form the curved roof sections—from sheets of plywood laid over steel frames. Then crews poured concrete into the molds. After the concrete had hardened, the molds were removed, and the heavy pieces were lifted by crane and moved to a storage area. Pieces continued to be formed in this way until workers had created more than two thousand roof segments of varying sizes.

Final assembly of the roof required giant tower cranes, which were special-ordered from France. The heavy concrete roof segments were raised by crane and lowered into place. When the pieces were within a few inches of their final position, men stood on scaffolding platforms and applied a thick, milklike epoxy glue using sticks and ordinary paint rollers. Then the sections were stressed, or pulled together and held tight with tensioned steel cables. As the roof slowly began to take shape, one observer likened it to building with a gigantic set of Legos.

A Sea of White Ceramic

As progress continued on the roof shells, workers began to prepare the ceramic tiles that would cover them. Utzon had wanted to achieve a special look with the tiles, which he describes: "A roof of white tiles would emphasise the sculptural character of the building. Particularly at night, when the pale violet glow of a Sydney night would make the structure glimmer in the dark. But this called for a ceramic tile . . . that would be per-

ceived as true stoneware and would simultaneously give an impression of brilliance as it reflected the light."[3] Utzon found exactly what he was looking for in Sweden, and special-ordered more than a million off-white ceramic tiles from a firm that was located there.

To prepare the tiles for application to the roof, crews used a unique process. A batch of tiles was laid

Tower cranes from France lowered more than two thousand concrete roof segments into place.

More than 1 million ceramic tiles, which were set in concrete sections, make up the opera house's roof.

face down in a mold, and concrete was poured over them. When the concrete dried, the mold was removed, leaving a concrete lid that could be attached to the roof sections. There were two reasons why this method of applying tiles was preferable. First, it ensured the most even application. Also, it was safer for workers because it eliminated the need for them to apply more than a million tiles while balancing on scaffolding. As a result of these safe practices, there were no fatal accidents during the building of the opera house roof.

In February 1966, cranes began hoisting the heavy tile lids high into the air, where they were fastened to the shells with bronze bolts and aluminum brackets. Utzon and Arup had planned for this work to start six months earlier; however, testing had shown the need for further adjustments and corrections, so the tiling process was delayed.

Trouble Brewing

The tile delay was only one of many setbacks that had occurred since work on the opera house had begun. From the very beginning, there were problems with everything from building the podium to the design and construction of the roof. As a result, a project that had been idealistically planned for completion in about five years was nowhere near finished. Some of these problems were caused by Utzon's designs, which were beautiful on paper but proved nearly impossible to construct. Arup engineer Jack Zunz explains: "Although Utzon's Opera House was the stuff that dreams are made of, although his use of shapes, materials, textures and colours was individual . . . I don't think that he ever really understood the complexity of the problems he was creating."[4]

These troubles and others led not only to extensive construction delays, but they also caused serious cost overruns. John Cahill's original ballpark estimate was $7 million, but the podium alone had cost nearly that much. By the middle of 1964, Utzon provided a revised quote of $35 million to government officials—and their reaction was one of shock and anger. Even though Utzon alone was not responsible for all the problems, they still blamed him.

In May 1965, a new government was elected in New South Wales. The new premier, Robert Askin, vowed to put an end to the delays and escalating costs that had plagued the opera house. He focused his attention on one man: Jørn Utzon. Askin suspended payment of Utzon's monthly retainer and refused to pay more than one hundred thousand dollars of his outstanding fees. Utzon, believing he had no other

Blamed for construction delays and huge cost overruns, Utzon resigned, left Australia, and never returned to see the completed structure.

choice, resigned as architect of the Sydney Opera House on February 28, 1966. Two months later, he and his family left Australia to return to their native Denmark.

Within two months of Utzon's resignation, a new team of men had replaced him. In April 1966, Davis Hughes, the government's newly appointed minister for public works, chose architects Peter Hall, Lionel Todd, and David Littlemore to assume responsibility for completion of the opera house.

To complete construction of the opera house, architects Peter Hall, Lionel Todd, and David Littlemore replaced Utzon.

Chapter 4

Stops and Starts

FROM THE VERY start, the new architectural team faced many challenges. Nine years had passed since Utzon's design was chosen, and since then the government had reconsidered how the opera house theaters would be used. After receiving new requirements from some major users of the facility, government officials determined that the original specifications were no longer adequate. Both the large and small theaters needed to be expanded, and other changes would also be necessary.

For the next two and a half years, Hall and his team worked with Arup to redesign the interior structure of the opera house. They also worked on designs for the building's immense glass walls, which proved to be nearly as challenging as the roof had been. Utzon had envisioned them as "hanging curtains of glass," and while Arup engineers agreed with his ideas in theory, they found it difficult to come up with a solution that

Opposite:
Construction of the Sydney Opera House, which faced unique challenges and troubles, took fourteen years to complete.

would work. By the time workers finished construct-ing the roof in early 1967, Arup was still nowhere near finalizing the design of the glass walls.

While plans for the interior of the building and the walls were still being developed, crews began covering the exposed concrete surfaces of the podium, a process known as cladding. This involved the application of prefabricated granite panels, three inches thick and in varying sizes, which Utzon had previously ordered from an Australian firm. The pinkish gray granite pan-els were also used to clad the steps of the grand staircase, as well as the broadwalk, which gave these surfaces a smooth, finished look.

Hanging Curtains of Glass

By early 1970, Arup's designs for the glass walls were finally complete. The engineers had decided to use laminated glass, which provided the greatest possible safety against breakage. After Arup determined how much glass was needed, it was special-ordered from a manufacturer in France. The glass came in oversize rectangular sheets, so Arup purchased custom-built sawing machines that could cut the required sizes and shapes. Altogether, about two thousand panels in seven hundred different sizes were needed for the glass walls.

Construction crews built supporting frames, called mullions, out of steel. Certain roof segments had previ-ously been designated as supports, and now the mullions were connected to these supports, bolted into place, and painted. Then it was time to install the glass,

a process known as glazing. The men first mounted bronze fixtures (or glazing bars) onto the mullions. Using mobile cranes with suction lifting equipment, they hoisted the glass panels up to the scaffolding plat-forms. Workers standing on the platforms positioned the glass panels onto the glazing bars and temporarily clamped the panels in place. The next step was to in-stall cover pieces, which were designed to permanently hold the glass panels onto the glazing bars. The cover pieces were installed and fastened tightly to the glazing bars with special brackets. This formed a "sandwich" of

More than sixty-seven thousand square feet of glass were used to make the hanging glass curtains.

the glazing bars, the glass panels, and the cover pieces. The workers' last step was to apply silicone rubber sealant to the joints, which provided a watertight seal.

In 1972, two years after crews started to build the glass walls, the work was finished. In the process, more than sixty-seven thousand square feet of glass were used—which was nearly enough to cover an entire city block.

The Finishing Touches

While the walls were being built, crews continued to work on the interiors. One particularly major undertaking was the electric wiring, because the amount of cable needed was astounding—more than four hundred miles (six hundred and forty-four kilometers) of electrical cable were used to power the opera house. When electricians had completed the wiring, the power in the facility was enough to provide electricity to an entire town of twenty-five thousand people.

Another item of major importance was an air-conditioning system that was large enough and powerful enough to ensure comfortable temperatures at all times. After the system had been installed, more than twelve miles of ductwork stretched throughout the building.

Also during the final construction phase, workers finished the interior walls, floors, and ceilings in the two theaters. In the large theater, known as the Concert Hall, workers built an orchestral platform and installed 2,690 audience seats. In the smaller hall, called the Opera Theatre, an orchestra pit was built and

The Concert Hall Grand Organ

On May 30, 1979, a spectacular instrument was unveiled in the Sydney Opera House: the Concert Hall grand organ. Designed by Ronald Sharp, a self-taught organ builder from Sydney, the huge pipe organ took twelve years to build and cost more than a million dollars.

Sharp's creation is a mechanical-action organ, which means the levers that operate it go directly from the keyboard to the pipes. By pressing the keys, the organist activates a series of levers, springs, and pushrods that allows air to flow to the pipes, thus controlling the sound. Sound can also be controlled when the organist opens and closes a series of knobs called stops. The pipes can produce very different sounds. The sounds may mimic reed, wind, or string instruments.

The Concert Hall grand organ has more than ten thousand pipes, grouped into two hundred rows called ranks, and 131 stops. It is the world's largest mechanical-action organ, and one of largest pipe organs in the world.

Sharp began to design the pipe organ in 1967, when the Concert Hall was still under construction. Two years later, he was awarded a contract to build the in-

The grand organ took twelve years to build and is one of the largest pipe organs in the world.

strument. When the opera house performed its first test concert in 1972, the organ was still seven years from completion, but one of Sharp's assistants demonstrated it for the audience. During the final months of construction, an Austrian organ-building firm called Gregor Hradetzsky worked with Sharp and his staff to finish building the organ. On June 7, 1979, the first recital featuring the organ was performed by Douglas Lawrence, an organist from Melbourne, Australia.

The Opera Theatre, the smaller of the two performance halls, seats more than fifteen hundred people.

1,547 audience seats were installed. In both theaters, acoustic systems were put in, as were a variety of stage equipment and sophisticated lighting systems.

Inside the podium, crews constructed the drama theater and a large rehearsal room that could double as a recording studio. They also built a smaller room where recitals or receptions could be held, a small cinema, and a seven-thousand-square-foot exhibition room. A number of other miscellaneous rooms were built inside the structure as well, including rehearsal rooms, lounges, and lavish dressing rooms for visiting artists.

By the winter of 1972, almost all work on the Sydney Opera House was complete and the final product was magnificent—but it had far exceeded budget and schedule estimations. Instead of taking five years to build, construction had dragged on for nearly fourteen years. And the final cost, which was originally estimated at $7 million, was actually $102 million.

Beautiful Music

Finally, it was time to test the facility's new acoustic system. On December 17, 1972, before an audience of construction workers and invited guests, the Sydney Symphony Orchestra performed for the first time in the Concert Hall. It was not an official grand opening, but it was no less magical to those who were part of it.

Author John Yeomans, who was in the audience, says everything about the day was perfect, and the sound in the Concert Hall was clear and beautiful. Yet he notes the glaring absence of the creative genius behind the opera house design—Jørn Utzon. Although the architect's name was not mentioned even once in the speeches given that day, Yeomans says it is Utzon who will forever be known as the true creator of the Sydney Opera House:

> I am sure that in twenty years time the names of all the able, and in some cases brilliant men who slaved to get the Opera House finished will have been forgotten and Utzon's name alone will remain in the public mind. . . . [The] strange word "Utzon" will be [permanently] linked with a building which will probably last longer than the pyramids. And that, I suppose, is as close to immortality as an architect can come.[5]

Australia's Dream Becomes a Reality

THE FIRST PUBLIC performance at the Sydney Opera House was held in the Opera Theatre on September 28, 1973. The Australian Opera Company performed *War and Peace,* a production of the famed Russian composer Sergey Prokofiev. The following night, the Sydney Symphony Orchestra gave a performance in the Concert Hall.

The "Beautiful Home" Is Opened

On October 20, 1973, England's Queen Elizabeth II officially opened the Sydney Opera House in a gala ceremony. The queen and her husband, the duke of Edinburgh, presided over the memorable event, which included a dazzling display of fireworks viewed by thousands of people around Sydney Harbor. After the celebration, a royal concert was performed by the

Opposite:
For more than thirty years, the Sydney Opera House has presented concerts, recitals, theater, ballet, and opera to more than 2 million people each year.

Sydney Symphony Orchestra. In the following weeks, hundreds of journalists from all over the world traveled to Sydney to see the opera house. One, a music critic from the *Los Angeles Times,* wrote about his impressions of the new facility: "This, without question, must be the most innovative, the most daring, the most dramatic and in many ways, the most beautiful home constructed for the lyric and related muses in modern times."[6]

The Opera House Today

Following the opera house opening, an area known as the Forecourt was built where Bennelong Point first starts to jut into Sydney Harbor. This work was completed in the late 1980s, and since then the Forecourt has been the site of many open-air concerts and events.

Also in the late 1980s, the broadwalk was extended and reconstructed, and a new lower-level concourse was built to house a variety of shops and restaurants.

In the early 1990s, the stage of the Concert Hall was expanded to provide more room for orchestra performances. Seating in all theaters was refurbished, and the orchestra pit in the Opera Theatre was enlarged to accommodate more musicians. Also, a new performance space called The Studio was built to host contemporary and modern performing arts.

Today, thirty years have passed since the Sydney Opera House opened its doors to the public. The facility has nearly a thousand rooms, including the theaters, five rehearsal studios, four restaurants, and six theater bars, as well as extensive foyer and lounge areas. There are also sixty dressing rooms, a library, an artists' lounge, offices, and extensive areas where machinery and equipment are housed. Each year the opera house presents more than two thousand performances including orchestra concerts, chamber music recitals, ballet and theatrical performances, and opera productions. With an annual audience of more than 2 million people, it is one of the busiest performing arts centers in the world.

Utzon's Final Triumph

When Jørn Utzon left Australia in 1966, he never returned, even to see the completion of his architectural masterpiece. During the ensuing years he rarely spoke publicly about his decision to resign, so most information about him was based on speculation rather than fact. Yet according to architect/author Philip Drew, "The Opera House crisis devastated Utzon. The project had meant so much to him."[7]

In 1992, the Royal Australian Institute of Architects honored Utzon with a commemorative medal for his work on the Sydney landmark—but even more significant was the official apology that accompanied the award. Then eleven years later, Utzon was given the highest honor an architect can receive: the Pritzker Architecture Prize, a lifetime achievement award given annually to one architect who has con-

The Sydney Opera House is the pride of Australia and has been called one of the Seven Wonders of the Modern World.

sistently shown talent, dedication, and commitment to architecture. Utzon received the prestigious award at a ceremony held at the Royal Academy of Fine Arts in Madrid, Spain, on May 20, 2003.

In addition to these honors, Utzon's architectural accomplishments were recognized in another very significant way. In 1999, he was appointed design consultant for the Sydney Opera House. In that capacity, he would guide all architectural activities related to the facility, including overseeing a proposed $24 million in renovations to the two theaters, glass walls, and other interior and exterior areas. For health-related reasons, Utzon could not travel to Sydney to personally supervise the project. Instead, he oversees and directs it from his home on the Spanish island of Majorca.

Sydney's Pride

The Sydney Opera House, which towers over the choppy blue waters of the harbor and the red-tiled roofs of Sydney, is the realization of a dream—one that began long ago with Eugene Goossens, and was brought to life by Jørn Utzon, Ove Arup, and many others who helped make the dream a reality. It is indeed the pride of Australia, as well as one of the great architectural treasures of the world. No one can sum up its importance better than the architect who created it nearly a half-century ago: "It has become such a marvellous thing . . . for Australia and for time. . . . Sometimes in architecture it happens that a daring step into the unknown gives us great gifts for the future."[8]

Notes

Introduction: A Building Ahead of Its Time

1. Quoted in Fergus Shiel and Giles Tremlett, "Utzon's Unfinished Symphony," *Age*, April 15, 2002. www.theage. com.au.

Chapter 1: In Search of the Perfect Design

2. Quoted in Ove Arup and Jack Zunz, "Sydney Opera House," *Arup Journal*, October 1973, pp. 4–5.

Chapter 3: A Stunning Building Comes to Life

3. Quoted in Françoise Fromonot, *Jørn Utzon: The Sydney Opera House*. Milan, Italy: Electa, 2000, p. 113.
4. Jack Zunz, "Introduction," *Arup Journal*, October 1973, p. 2.

Chapter 4: Stops and Starts

5. John Yeomans, *The Other Taj Mahal: What Happened to the Sydney Opera House*. Camberwell, Australia: Longman, 1973, p. 216.

Chapter 5: Australia's Dream Becomes a Reality

6. Quoted in *Sydney Opera House*, "Storylines: Sydney Opera House—the Site, the Story and the Building." www.sydney operahouse.com.
7. Philip Drew, *Sydney Opera House: Jørn Utzon*. London: Phaidon, 1995, p. 23.
8. Quoted in Anne Maria Nicholson, "Sydney Opera House Project," ABC Online, transcript from radio interview with Jørn Utzon, July 8, 2002. www.abc.net.

Chronology

1946	Eugene Goossens begins to lobby for a performance facility in Sydney.
1954	Premier John Joseph Cahill appoints a committee to investigate having an opera house built; the committee selects Bennelong Point as the site and plans an international design competition.
1956	The design competition is publicly announced.
1957	Judging takes place; Cahill announces Jørn Utzon as the winner.
1958	Wrecking crews demolish an old railroad building on Bennelong Point to make way for the opera house.
1959	Cahill and Utzon preside over a ceremony to mark the start of construction; seven months later, Cahill dies.
1963	The podium is complete and work begins on the roof.
1966	Utzon resigns as architect of the Sydney Opera House and returns with his family to Denmark; two months later, a new team of architects is chosen to take his place.
1967	Workers finish applying the last of the tile lids to the opera house roof.
1970	Work begins on the third phase of construction: the interior work and the glass walls.
1972	The glass walls and most interior work is complete; an orchestra concert is performed for construction workers and invited guests in the Concert Hall.
1973	The first public performance at the opera house is held in the Opera Theatre; a grand opening celebration is held; England's Queen Elizabeth II officially opens the Sydney Opera House.
1992	The Royal Australian Institute of Architects honors Utzon with a commemorative medal and an official apology.
1999	Utzon is appointed design consultant for the Sydney Opera House to oversee all future architectural activities related to the facility.
2003	Utzon is honored with the coveted Pritzker Architecture Prize.

Glossary

bedrock—solid rock that is found far beneath the soil.

cladding—any coating that is bonded to a particular surface.

formwork—forms or molds that contain and shape wet concrete.

glazing—the process of installing glass.

mullions—metal frames, or metal strips, that divide and hold panes of glass.

podium—the tiered granite-clad concrete platform that serves as the foundation for the Sydney Opera House.

Pritzker Architecture Prize—an esteemed award given annually to an architect who has consistently shown talent, dedication, and commitment to the field of architecture.

scaffolding—a temporary metal frame built to support workers and materials during a construction project.

sphere—a round figure whose points are all the same distance from the center.

stress—to exert pressure on something.

tower crane—a machine capable of lifting extremely heavy objects hundreds of feet in the air.

vault—a concrete roof whose structure is based on an arch or curve.

For More Information

Books

Reg Cox, *The Seven Wonders of the Modern World.* Parsippany, NJ: Silver Burdett, 1996.

John Yeomans, *The Other Taj Mahal: What Happened to the Sydney Opera House.* Camberwell, Australia: Longman, 1973.

Oswald Leopold Ziegler, *Sydney Builds an Opera House.* Sydney: Oswald Ziegler, 1973.

Web Site

Sydney Opera House (www.sydneyoperahouse.com). An excellent site that is both informative and interesting. Includes the history of the opera house, as well as stories, descriptions of events that are held at the facility, and a virtual "tour" that allows site visitors to get a firsthand look at the building inside and out. Also features a special section especially designed for young people.

About the Author

Peggy J. Parks holds a bachelor of science degree from Aquinas College in Grand Rapids, Michigan, where she graduated magna cum laude. She is a freelance writer who has written numerous books for Gale Group imprints, including Blackbirch Press, KidHaven Press, and Lucent Books. She was also the profile writer for *Grand Rapids: The City That Works,* a book produced by Towery Publications. Parks lives in Muskegon, Michigan, a town she says inspires her writing because of its location on the shores of Lake Michigan.

Index

Aborigines, 13
acoustic system, 36, 37
air-conditioning, 34
Arup, Ove, 12, 18, 20, 23, 31, 32, 43
Askin, Robert, 28

Bennelong Point, 10, 12, 13, 15, 17, 40
broadwalk, 19, 32, 40

Cahill, John, 10, 14–15, 15
ceramic tiles, 6, 24–27
Concert Hall, 34, 35, 37, 41
concrete, 18, 19, 24, 26
cost overruns, 27–28

Forecourt, 40

glass walls, 15, 31–34
glazing, 32–34
Goossens, Eugene, 9–10, 15, 43

Hall, Peter, 29, 31
hanging curtains, of glass, 31–34

Littlemore, David, 29
lottery, 14–15

mullions, 32–33

New South Wales, 5, 13

Opera Theatre, 34, 39, 41
organ, 35

Phillip, Arthur, 13
pillars, 20, 21
podium, 11, 15, 18–20, 36
Pritzker Architecture Prize, 42

roof, 6, 7, 12, 15, 19–21, 23–27

sandstone, 17
scaffolding, 23
Seven Wonders of the Modern World, 5
staircase, 10, 15, 19, 32
Sydney Opera House audience at, 41
costs of, 27–28, 37
design competition for, 10–12
financing of, 14–15
foundation of, 19
grand opening of, 39–40
problems with, 17–18, 20, 27–29
redesign of, 31
renovations to, 40, 43
today, 40–41
weight of, 6, 20, 21
Sydney Symphony Orchestra, 9, 37, 39, 40

tiles, ceramic, 6, 24–27
Todd, Lionel, 29

Utzon, Jørn, 10–12, 15, 18, 19, 20–21, 24–25, 27, 28–29, 37, 41–43

walls, glass, 15, 31–34
wind, 12, 20, 21
wiring, 34